In

Flight

with

David

McPhail

written and
illustrated
by
David
McPhail

CREATIVE · SPARKS

from HEINEMANN

In Flight with

DAVID McPHAIL

· A CREATIVE AUTOBIOGRAPHY ·

HEINEMANN
Portsmouth, NH

Heinemann
A division of Reed Elsevier Inc.
361 Hanover Street
Portsmouth, NH 03801-3912

Offices and agents throughout the world

We would like to thank those who have given their permission to include material in this book. Credits for borrowed material appear on page 41.

Library of Congress Cataloging-in-Publication Data
McPhail, David M.
In flight with David McPhail / David McPhail.
p. cm.— (Creative Sparks)
Summary: The author describes how he goes about the process of writing and illustrating books.
ISBN 0-435-08132-2
1. McPhail, David—Juvenile literature. 2. Authors, American—20th century—Biography—Juvenile literature. 3. Illustrators—United States—Biography—Juvenile literature. 4. Children's stories—Authorship—Juvenile literature. 5. Illustration of books—Juvenile literature. [1. McPhail, David. 2. Authors, American. 3. Illustrators. 4. Authorship. 5. Illustration of books.] I. Title. II. Series.
PS3563.C38865Z466 1996
813'.54—dc20
[B] 95-40132 CIP AC

Editor: Carolyn Coman
Text and cover design: Virginia Evans, EvansDay Design

Printed on acid-free paper
99 98 97 96   RRD   1 2 3 4 5 6

Printed in Mexico

For

sister

Sue,

with

love

've always loved to draw. I loved
to draw when I was a young child,
and I still love to draw as a middle-aged
man. I've drawn thousands—even tens
of thousands—of pictures, sometimes the
same one over and over, but I still love
doing it.

The first drawings I ever did were on pieces of brown paper bags that my grandmother cut up for me. I drew with a fat black crayon just right for my chubby little fingers.

I can remember loading up my Radio Stake wagon with drawings I had done and taking them over to my girlfriend's house. I think her mother burned them.

Years later, I wrote a story called *The Magical Drawings of Moony B. Finch* about a little boy who loved to draw. Moony was me—or more to the point, Moony was who I wanted to be. Moony could draw so well that his drawings came to life.

Mine never did.

In a way I don't mind. My drawings require more from the viewer's imagination—which is perhaps how it should be.

Sometimes I feel as though I write words just to go with the pictures that dance through my head. (The pictures I see in my head are fuzzy and out of focus. *That's why I draw them*—so I can better see what they look like. If those images in my head were sharp and vivid, I'd have no need to draw them.) I don't think of myself as a writer. Stories just seem to come to me. I write only after I feel a prickly sensation stirring in my brain. By now I know this means there's a story in there trying to get out.

I'm convinced that stories find me, not the other way around—and if I'm not prepared, they move on, perhaps never to return. That's why I try to be ready. I always have pen and paper nearby. Some stories come rather quickly and easily. I feel as though a voice is telling me the story and all I have to do is write it down. (Sometimes I have a hard time keeping up.)

That happened with a story about a bear named Henry—
Henry Bear's Park. I wrote the story when I was living on Cape
Cod. I was expecting friends from Boston to visit one afternoon.
I built a fire in the fireplace, and while I was waiting for my
friends to show up, I started writing.

The idea had been swimming around in my mind for a few
days, but, as is true with most of my stories, I didn't know much
beyond the first line or two. So I began. "Henry Bear lived in a
cozy house near the center of a small town." One sentence
followed another, and soon I was scribbling furiously.

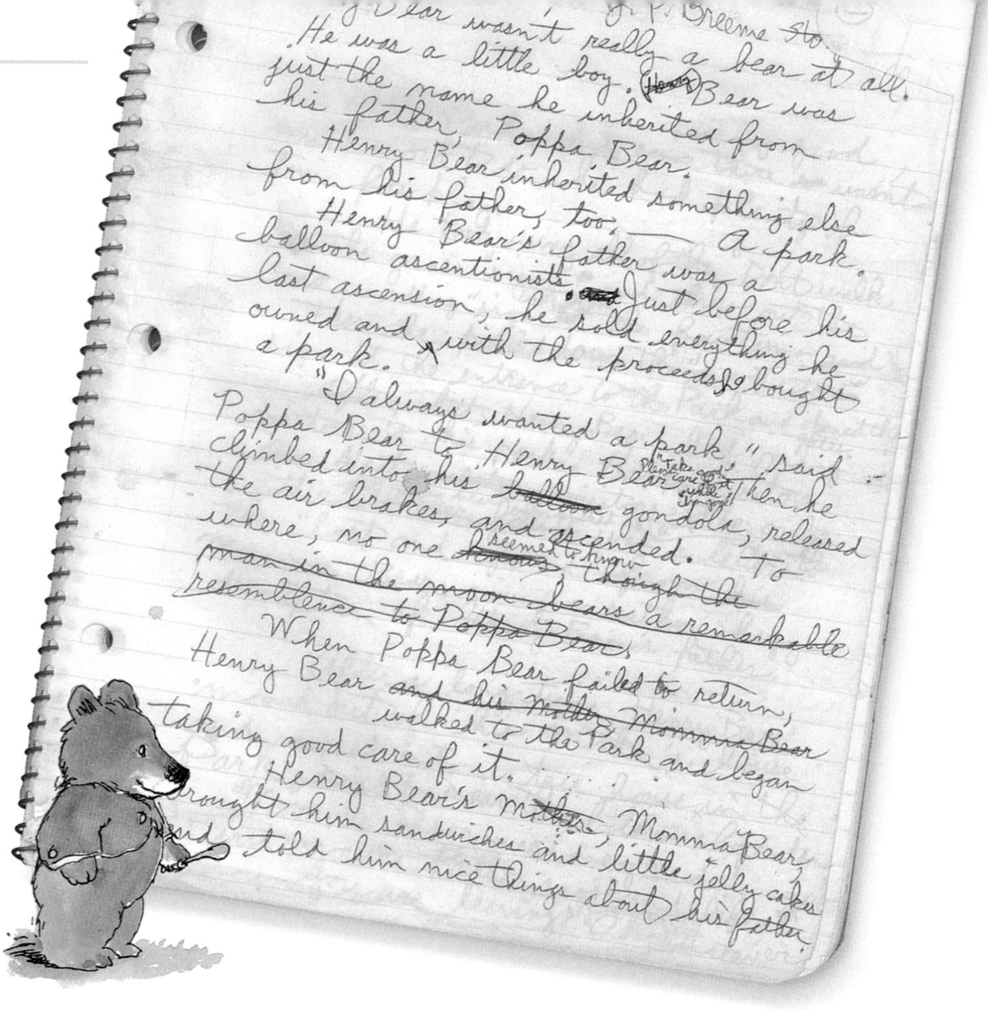

[handwritten notebook draft]

...Bear wasn't really a bear at all. He was a little boy. Henry Bear was just the name he inherited from his father, Poppa Bear.

Henry Bear inherited something else from his father, too, — a park. Henry Bear's father was a balloon ascensionist. Just before his last ascension, he sold everything he owned and with the proceeds bought a park.

"I always wanted a park," said Poppa Bear to Henry Bear. Then he climbed into his balloon gondola, released the air brakes, and ascended to where, no one seemed to know, though the man in the moon bears a remarkable resemblance to Poppa Bear.

When Poppa Bear failed to return, Henry Bear and his mother, Momma Bear walked to the park and began taking good care of it. Henry Bear's mother, Momma Bear brought him sandwiches and little jelly cakes and told him nice things about his father.

About half an hour later there came a knock at the door. My friends from the city had arrived. I threw open the door—startling them, I'm sure—and said, "I'm in the middle of writing something. Go to the beach and come back in an hour!" And I slammed the door closed again. When they returned an hour later, the story was finished.

Other stories seem to play games with me—sort of "hide and seek." I'll be writing along and suddenly the story disappears. The voice telling it goes silent and I'm left to figure it out on my own.

don't write at home or in my studio. I guess I feel that at home I should be doing "homey" things, like fixing supper, cleaning mirrors, feeding cats, watching TV, reading the newspaper, or talking to someone in my family. And at my studio I have the overpowering urge to draw or paint; writing is an unwanted intrusion.

So I go out.

I can "write" while driving my car. (Actually, what I do is think of a line or two, then pull over to the side of the road and write them down.) It's a slow method of getting anywhere, but some of my favorite stories have come while I've been driving. I wrote *The Cereal Box* this way. What was ordinarily a ninety-minute trip became a three-and-a-half-hour journey.

Another place I go to write is the local coffee shop. Even with all the hubbub swirling around me, I can write.

Then there's the old standby, the library. Our town library has many tables and chairs scattered among its book stacks, and I often sit for hours in a hidden corner, writing away.

This is how it works with me: I write the story longhand, on a pad of paper. Then I type it up (double spaced) and send it to the editor. It is the editor's job to help the writer write the best possible story.

Everything I write does not get published. I've written stories that I like a lot but no one else seems to, so they go into my file drawer for STORIES NOT YET PUBLISHED.

My first "pig" story has never been published. It's called *Pig Pig Farewell*. It's about an old pig who gives away all of his possessions and rows off into the sunset in a small boat. My editor, Emilie McLeod, thought it was a sad and tragic story—the pig was going off to die. I thought it was a hopeful story—the pig was going away to start a new life.

Anyway, even though she decided not to publish the story, Emilie was intrigued by the pig. She wanted to know more about him. "What was he like as a child?" she asked.

Out of that came *Pig Pig Grows Up*, followed by *Pig Pig Rides*, *Pig Pig and the Magic Photo Album*, and *Pig Pig Gets a Job*.

Ever since I read *Charlotte's Web*,
by E. B. White, I've wanted to
own a pig—a live pig. But I never
have, even though I've lived on
farms for a good part of my
adult life. Maybe I've drawn
pigs as a way of making up
for not having one.

Another animal I draw frequently is the bear. The Christmas I was two, I was given a big stuffed teddy bear. Teddy was his name. Teddy is probably one of the reasons I draw so many bears. I loved that bear. He's still around somewhere.

But back to books: If the editor decides to publish the story (that is, make a book out of it), we agree on "terms"—how much money I will be paid and when I am to deliver the finished manuscript. When the terms are settled, we sign a contract and get to work.

The editor returns the story with suggestions for changes to make it better. I, of course, feel that it's perfect as it is, but eventually I begin to see that perhaps it could stand some improvement. Back and forth the story goes until we both like it.

Erasers

soft

Hard

Pencil

Ink Pen

Fountain Pen

Ink Bottle

Brushes

Watercolor Box

Then it's time to draw the pictures.

Tools are what I call my drawing stuff (pencils, pens, brushes, paints, inks) and surfaces to draw on (paper, board, canvas). You don't need fancy equipment to make a drawing. There are pencils that cost a dollar each and there are those that cost a nickel. They both work. One day, at a yard sale, I bought a dozen or so pencils that were exactly like the ones I used in the fourth grade. I still draw with those pencils. I also use a penholder that was my grandfather's, and I buy nibs (points) wherever I can find them. A few years ago a friend gave me an inkwell for my birthday. I fill it with ink, dip the pen point into the ink, and draw.

I sit on a stool in front of a big drawing table. The table is old and scarred. It once belonged to a famous illustrator who used it during the late 1800s and early 1900s.

Good lighting is important. Attached to one corner of my drawing table is a lamp that I can adjust to illuminate whatever I am working on.

Before I begin each new book, I go through the ritual of cleaning off my table.

As the book progresses, the table gets more and more cluttered, so that by the time I'm finished, there's barely room to draw. There will be piles of sketchbooks, reference books, letters from editors and art directors, jars of brushes, a tray of paints, unwashed coffee mugs, plates covered with cookie or cracker crumbs, and assorted other things. (Once my baseball glove spent the entire off-season on my desk.)

When I begin to illustrate a new book I start by reading the story over and over, so that it's very familiar to me and I don't have to refer to it all the time.

Then I start doing little sketches. These are sometimes called "thumbnail" sketches because they are so small.

I often draw the same scene
many different ways—up close, far
away, from below, from above,
front view, rear view, and so forth.

I explore every possibility, then choose the one I like best.

At the same time I begin to develop the characters in the story and how they will look. Are they "cartoony," like Pig Pig, or are they "realistic," like the boy and his family that I painted for *Farm Boy's Year*?

Often I need to learn about people or
animals in different parts of the world, or
from another time in history. This is when
I go with my sketchbook to the library and
look up what I need to know.

I might fill a dozen sketch-books before I'm ready to start the final art—the drawings or paintings that will be seen in the published book.

efore I do the final art for a book I make what is called a "dummy." A dummy is a sort of homemade book that is the same size and shape as the published book will be.

Most of my books are thirty-two pages long. That means I have thirty-two pages to fill with my story and my drawings.

Sometimes I do more than one drawing for a page, and other times I do one drawing that covers two pages. It all depends on what I feel the story calls for. On average I probably do around two dozen separate pieces of art to fill the thirty-two pages.

The dummy is usually roughly drawn and is just a way of giving everyone involved in the making of the book (the editor, the art director, the printer, and of course me, the artist) a clear idea of what the book will look like.

"Will you draw something just for me?" asked the man. "Like a pirate's treasure chest filled with gold coins?"

"That's easy!" said Moony, and with a few quick strokes of his crayon it was done.

When he handed the drawing to the man the treasure chest slid right off the paper and landed in the man's lap!

Gold coins spilled out of the chest and rolled down the sidewalk attracting a large crowd.

The crowd murmured... ...then buzzed... then charged angrily right at Moony.

Taking his second piece of paper, Moony drew the fiercest dragon that he could imagine.

Moony tossed the drawing into the crowd, and when someone

touched the paper, the dragon immediately sprang to life... Roaring and breathing fire!

All the people ran for their lives! Even the bearded Old Man was gone in a flash.

With the crowd gone, the dragon turned on Moony.

Moony, meanwhile, had taken his third piece of paper and drawn a perfect likeness of the fierce dragon.

Taking his eraser once more he calmly began to erase...

The dummy usually gets sent back and forth many times before the final art is begun, for everyone involved usually has suggestions on how to make it better. I may have designed a page that shows a distant scene, with the central characters mere specks on the horizon. The editor and the art director may wish to see the characters close up—"Let's see what they look like."

I think about their suggestions and either do the drawing over or stick with my original idea. Since I'm the one who has to sit and do the drawing, the deciding factor is whether I can do it with conviction and energy. I have the final say because this is my book and in the end it has to be the way I want it to be. After all, it's my name on the cover. Usually my relationship with the other people who work on the book is a good one. We all want the same thing—a good book!

ventually the dummy is satisfactory to everyone, and it's time to begin the finished art. By now the "style" of art has been decided, as well as the "medium" (pencil, pen and ink, brush and paint, crayon, whatever). Most of the illustrations in my books are watercolors painted over an ink drawing.

I select a paper—it has to be thick enough so that it won't buckle when the watercolor is applied—and then I rough out the drawing with pencil. Often it takes several attempts to get the image right, so I make liberal use of my eraser at this stage.

When I'm satisfied with the pencil drawing, I take up the pen and carefully (but confidently) draw in the lines in ink. I don't try to trace the pencil lines; I just use them for a guide. When all of the essential pen lines have been drawn, I let the ink dry; then, with a soft eraser called a "kneaded" eraser, I vigorously erase all of the pencil lines. After the pencil lines are gone, I am ready to paint.

By now I have decided what the colors will be, so this stage is very much like painting a coloring book. I do my best to stay within the lines and to apply the paint neatly.

When I finish painting, I cover the art with a piece of tracing paper to keep it clean while I do the rest of the drawings.

When I do a good drawing, I feel wonderful, and all is right with the world. But when I try to get what I want on the paper without success, I'm devastated. I begin to feel that I've lost whatever small ability I once had.

When I was illustrating *Henry Bear's Park,* I worked late into the night, trying to create the illusion that rain was falling on this silly bear as he insisted on making music. Finally I was too tired to continue. I knew that if I kept working I risked ruining the picture, but I still wasn't sure that my scratchings looked like rain. Nevertheless, I went to bed, leaving the drawing uncovered on my drawing table.

I hadn't been asleep for very long
when I felt someone nudging me, and
heard a familiar voice calling softly,
"Daddy . . . Daddy . . . wake up."

I opened my eyes. There was my five-
year-old son, Tristian, holding the
drawing up to my face. "Henry Bear
playing music in the rain," he said
excitedly. "It's good!"

I smiled, kissed him, and went back
to sleep, a sleep of blissful contentment.

When I am finished with all the drawings for a book, I carefully pack them up and take them (or send them) to the publisher. Unless there are corrections or changes to be made, at this point my job is finished. It will be about six months before I see the results of my efforts. Usually I am pleased, occasionally I am disappointed. (Sometimes I feel I could have done a better job.)

've written and illustrated nearly fifty books, and done the illustrations for another fifteen or so that I didn't write. Some years I do as many as five books; other years I might do only one or two. My goal is to do perhaps one a year, even one every two years, so that I will be able to take the time I need and make the pictures truly special. For me, the most important thing is the process, not the results.

If the day ever comes when I find making books either boring or tedious, I hope I have the wisdom to quit and find another line of work. But the way things are going, I don't see that happening any time soon. I love to write and draw pictures, and I get paid to do it.

You can't beat that!

Credits